"This exquisitely crafted work of poetic and perennial wisdom reflects Gunilla's gift as a creative artist and spiritual teacher who has lived a life of kindness. These words distill profound spiritual truths into a prism of practices accessible to each of us and relevant to unify our splintered world."

ELLEN WINGARD, *Leadership for Social Impact, World Pulse Media*

"Gunilla Norris's little book is profoundly delicious and nourishing in every way. The wisdom is stunning—and we recognize it as truth right away. This book joins a handful of others that will be forever next to my bed for solace, for sweetness, for food. The book is, itself, an act of great kindness."

STEPHEN COPE, *author of The Great Work of Your Life*

"Norris's words, though simple, are rich with grace. Each brief meditation, light as meringue, is nevertheless laden with psychological and spiritual nurture—real food for the soul. Kindness never was so beautifully rendered as a spiritual path, an everyday practice, an evolutionary possibility."

KATHLEEN NOONE DEIGNAN, CND, PHD,
Professor of Religious and Environmental Studies,
Iona College

"*Great Love in Little Ways* can be a daily reader. I can imagine a person taking it up as the good news and carrying the thought, image, or prayer throughout the day. This little book is proudly simple and simply profound—let it take you to a deeper awareness of life on the path to kindness."

FATHER CARL J. ARICO, *founding member of Contemplative Outreach, priest of the Archdiocese of Newark, author of A Taste of Silence*

GREAT LOVE IN LITTLE WAYS

Reflections on the Power of Kindness

GUNILLA NORRIS

TWENTY-THIRD PUBLICATIONS

twentythirdpublications.com

For three dear friends who live their kindness

GRETA SIBLEY

JOYCE SIEVERS

MARCIA VAN DYCK

TWENTY-THIRD PUBLICATIONS
One Montauk Avenue, Suite 200 • New London, CT 06320
(860) 437-3012 or (800) 321-0411 • www.twentythirdpublications.com

Cover image: iStockphoto.com / Simona Osterman

ISBN: 978-1-62785-429-0
Library of Congress Control Number: 2019940113
Printed in the U.S.A.

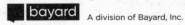
A division of Bayard, Inc.

CONTENTS

Where there is great love there are always miracles.

WILLA CATHER

Note to the Reader

Here in New England, where I live, you can walk its beautiful beaches and find pieces of sea glass. Those pieces have been tossed in the ocean. Their sharp edges are gone, and they are no longer able to cut your fingers. When you hold them up to the sun they reflect light through their many colors: yellow, white, green, purple, blue, and very rarely red.

The reflections in this little book are like those pieces of sea glass. There is nothing brand new written here. Experience has tumbled all the edges off. Yet I hope these perceptions can emit light. Gathered together they make a kaleidoscope you can use where the light of your own eyes and consciousness will shine through the reading of them, adding a new pattern and sparkle.

We may know many things with our minds. That does not mean we can embody what we know. Living a desire to be kind is like being tumbled in the ocean. Our sharp edges get worn away. We realize how small we are. It is good to own our limits, but the light of kindness has no limits. It is vast. It can shine through us in its own ways.

This book appears to be organized in a certain way: being kind to ourselves, being kind to others, and cultivating a steady state of kindness. This is not a sequential process, however, but a kind of simultaneity. Just as in a kaleidoscope, all the pieces are there turning with the light. We are always being relational in a much vaster way than we know when kindness is our path.

My hope is that this book will be your friend, and that its edges will be worn by frequent use. May it encourage you. May it shine a little light on the ways you want to dwell in and cultivate kindness.

INTRODUCTION

Imagine a kaleidoscope in your hands. Gazing through the glass you can see colorful pieces that make a lovely pattern. By turning the kaleidoscope just a little, the pieces fall into a new pattern. Almost at once something new is there to behold.

We gaze out at the world all the time and see patterns that are often thoughtless and cruel. The amazing thing is that we can change those patterns by turning our perception just a little toward kindness: a smile, a helping hand, a gentle word of encouragement, a bit of patience, and always the slow, inward growth toward wholeness and love. These are ways that can help to change our hardened, old patterns. Everything we have ever been is still useful if we turn the glass and see things from the perspective of kindness.

Tiny ways of growing more conscious and expressing kindness point us to something much larger than any one of us can fathom. As much as the air we breathe, the water we drink, the earth we stand upon, and the sunlight that warms us, we need kindness. It is the fifth element that knits us together and sustains us.

We forget how central kindness is to existence. Without water, we would die. Without human kindness, given and received, we would soon perish. We need to recognize this truth, to value it, and to practice it.

We know we will fail to be kind on many occasions when we wanted to be so. Old habits of self-protection and judgment overtake us with surprising force. It is as if the old animal instinct to survive at any cost reasserts itself. From primitive times our brains were wired to look for what was wrong and could harm us. To this day our brains continue to have that kind of vigilance. But our brains have also evolved and have learned to look for what is kind, and for what will help us, as well as what will help others. As a species we are all able to be more aware, to change, to transform, and to contribute. This is evolutionary.

Mother Teresa said that *we cannot do great things, but we can do little things with great love*. We can do so best over time by being constant, conscious, and caring in small ways. Learning to live in this humble way will change us at the core and create a pattern we can follow. In it we will be re-patterned to be not only human but also humane.

Whether directed to ourselves or to someone else, an attitude of kindness has the power to gentle and to slow the speed at which we live our lives. In its embrace we become more mindful, more effective, and more loving. It is no surprise that mindfulness creates kindness. Being fully present and genuine, we lose nothing in sharing small acts of kindness. We are just lighting another person's candle with our flame. Nothing is lost. Only more light is gained.

REFLECTIONS ON SELF-KINDNESS

Good people, most royal
greening verdancy
rooted in the sun, you shine
with radiant light.

HILDEGARD OF BINGEN

THE SUNSHINE IN YOUR FACE

All of us know the feeling of a polite smile, or the smile we use when we have been hurt and need to cover up our feelings. We know the party smile that begins to ache after an hour or two. Then there is the have-a-nice-day smile that is automatic, not unlike a handshake that will not be remembered.

What is a real smile? Is it not a lifting of the heart—making recognition and participation visible on our faces, for we cannot help but smile when something has reached our inner being? Our smiles join us to the goodness in the world.

There are therapies that ask people to smile, even if they don't feel like it. Science has proven that when we smile, we are sending an astounding amount of helpful messages to the chemistry in our bodies. We actually warm up the endocrine system. It may seem artificial, but if we smiled at our image in the mirror every morning even if it is a bad day, we will soon sense the self-kindness we have generated. It is a bit like a kindness bank account. We will find the balance growing. Haven't we noticed that the kindest people are those who think nothing of it? They have a fortune.

When two people genuinely smile on one another, they create a mutual radiance. Imagine what this might be like if there were hundreds of thousands of people smiling on one another this way. The world would glow.

A genuine smile is kindness made visible. It is a sign of welcome. It is the good in goodwill. It is sunshine in your face.

*The eye through which I see God is
the same eye through which God sees me;
my eye and God's eye are one eye, one
seeing, one knowing, one love.*

MEISTER ECKHART

PLAIN SEEING

One of the most wonderful and tender ways
to navigate in the world is to see it plainly,
without adding opinions to what we see. It is
a kindness practice that will never be over if
we decide to embark on it.

We may choose to look at something, a blue
sweater, for instance. When we see the sweater without adding anything—such as, *that's an
ugly blue sweater*, or *that's a gorgeous blue sweater*—we are simply seeing it. The sweater can
be what it is, without being layered over with

qualifications. We are so used to adding eval-
uation to our seeing that we don't even know
we are doing it. Suppose for a single hour we
decided to catch ourselves at it. We would be
amazed at how much we judge and evaluate
even the most ordinary parts of our lives. To
see and let things be what they simply are is a
holy way to see.

We will never know what something really
is, whether it is a tree, a cat, or a human being.
We can only be *with* the tree, the cat, or the
human. Being *with* is a different kind of seeing.
Dropping our automatic opinions frees us,
and everything else, to be what it is. We will
be liberated from constantly trying to improve
things or disparage them.

One hour of simply seeing is an adventure
into freedom and inner kindness. In essence,
it is simple, but it is not easy. If we would like
to experiment with this, we can cover our eyes
with our hands. We can warm them, appreciate the gift of them, and intend to see without
opinions for a morning. We would notice how

images enter our eyes. The images are for that moment inside us. The eyes let the images in without our conscious consent. We are in the world and the world we see is inside us. This is actually objective and a clean, sacred way of seeing.

The smallest thing
will not be forgotten.
JULIAN OF NORWICH

TAKING REFUGE

Safe places are places of refuge and nourishment. A safe place can be an actual location or a relationship that we count on and trust. A safe place can be a strong belief system or a discipline we are committed to. Having a refuge and taking refuge keeps us steady as we grow and unfold.

Kindness is a refuge and is found everywhere if we would just notice: the door that is opened for us, the smile for no reason, the offered ear, the comforting word. Such random acts happen in the trillions. Kindness is built into us as part of being human, and we are remiss to take it for granted.

Beginning with ourselves, what refuge in kindness can we offer our bodies? More rest? Less food? Time spent in nature? A warm, comforting bath? Understood as kindness, these small things become much bigger. They become lived regard, a steady caretaking we give to ourselves. Our homes need kindness too: keeping order, dusting the furniture, sweeping the floors, changing the sheets, and watering the plants. Doing the household chores in the spirit of kindness will make our homes into sanctuaries.

Refuge does not mean avoidance of the world, other people, and the challenges that are part of living. Cultivating kindness means we are taking the refuge of it with us everywhere we go. Think how a snail moves over the ground feeling everything as it travels. We can be that close to our circumstances, feeling our way forward in a kind of living Braille. Living that closely and intimately with what we encounter is a brave way to live. We can do it when, like the snail, we have the home of kindness at our back, a space to withdraw where there is refuge from reactivity. It is a wordless state of being, and it will always be available.

In the end only three things matter:
how much you loved, how gently you lived,
and how gracefully you let go of
things not meant for you.

THE BUDDHA

LETTING GO

As we mature we let go of childhood. This happens naturally. We let go of one day to make room for another. We let go of seasons and years. We don't even think about it. But to let go of resentments is another thing entirely. Holding on for dear life the way barnacles do, we won't let go of dreams that meant the world to us and are no longer possible. Letting go of the ways we judge ourselves is nigh impossible. We know, we know, we know to let go, but to do it is another thing.

To love much and to live gently is really a process of continually letting go of what is not meant for us. Preferences and desires are natural. It is our identification with them that is unnatural and causes suffering. Here is an example. *I hate mayonnaise. I am a mustard kind of person.* This shows identification with a preference. It signals the thought: *I am my preference.* Apply this to self-judgments or inner demands and we have created suffering. Self-definition of this kind narrows the world and constrains our ability to grow and to live fully.

To live fully is to continually be in process and change. We are like streams of intention and energy. These streams are directed by our thoughts and circumstances. Because we are created particular, there are things for us to be about. Life needs us to engage in them and to let go of that which is not meant for us. Asking *Is this mine?* is a wonderful discerning habit to develop.

It is such a simple little question, but it is hot and cuts through the ways we cling to our preferences—and curiously also to what we dislike. In a way it is a conscience question. Sorting in this way is not something we think; it is something we know deeply in our gut. When we live in accordance with the answers we receive from that level, we will have richer and more meaningful lives. What belongs to us lets us live Big and nurtures others as well. Everything we have is really on loan. We will have to let all of it go. The only thing that is ours is to have lived meaningfully, doing what was ours to do.

Whoever does not, sometime or other,
give full consent, full "joyous" consent,
to the dreadfulness of life, can never
take possession of the unutterable
abundance and power of our existence,
can only walk on its edge...

RAINER MARIA RILKE

ENDINGS

Endings will always be with us. How we leave a relationship, a long commitment, or a work situation sets the tone of how our next unfolding will begin. Truly ending something, not just letting it go for the moment, can be a blessing and a terror at the same time. Saying a last goodbye hurts, and it costs. Sometimes it might even feel like an amputation.

What we once had might have been wonderful, and yet it is over. We must leave it. Somehow, we know that if we do not say that final goodbye, we will wither inside, and eventually the withering will show up on the outside as well.

To say goodbye is to abandon the familiar. Goodbye stands for *God be with you*. We abandon the person or the situation to the love and companionship of God. When we do that with a burning heart, we will act out of deep honesty. Honesty is the cleanest kindness and ultimately the most tender one, although that may not be apparent at first.

And what of the reverse, when we are abandoned, when the goodbye is meant for us? The reverberation in our lives may feel like an earthquake, the ground gaping open at our feet, ready to swallow us. *God be with me* can be a needed, last-ditch prayer on the receiving end of a last goodbye.

Whether at a deathbed, at the last stop on the railroad line, or the haunting sound of the dial tone when the phone is hung up, the radical abandonment of ourselves or another into God's keeping is a fundamental act of kindness. We must make the truth of ending one of surrender. It may take a long time to feel that God is with you and me in those situations, but even a small understanding can be a blessing and a release. On the surface it looks like such a very little thing. In the depth of our being, it is big. We have begun to live again. When a storm has brought down branches, littering the ground with leaves and debris, a clear sky will follow. We are invited to begin again, to clean up our lives, and to trust. That is kindness, and it is fierce.

What are you waiting for?
Isn't it already here waiting for you?

ANONYMOUS

WAITING

Tapping feet, fingers drumming on the table top, watching water that will not boil fast enough, the fixed stare at the kitchen clock where the minute hand crawls slowly round and round: these are the telltale signs of tortured waiting. We want what we want before we can have it, or we dread what we expect, and want to avoid what we think is coming.

To have the capacity to wait in trust and leisure is to be wrapped in kindness the way a child is in the womb, growing slowly at the right pace. Or it may be the way a bulb lies peacefully in the ground, gathering enough strength to emerge. Time is not then an enemy, but a gift that allows things to come to fruition.

When we crack the egg before the chick is ready, it will be handicapped. It may never be able to fly. Patience is not a life sentence. It is life lived in a certain spirit. It is possible to cease impatient waiting and instead *wait upon* the events in our lives and the longings of our hearts. It is the spirit of kindness that holds things gently in time. It is not finger drumming, but more like two hands holding each other in solidarity.

We have many chances to wait: at the checkout counter in the grocery store, in the doctor's office, or in a weekend's traffic jam. Nothing can happen then except waiting. These are the in-between times, when, if we grow to appreciate them, give us space away from our agendas. We are given time for time—moments to rest from effort, and to look beyond the immediacy we think is so important. Our souls can catch up with our bodies. The sense of somehow knowing that something will eventually come to fruition, and the knowing of not knowing anything, can meet. That meeting is filled with dynamic trust. It loves and allows for days of incubation.

We can then see beyond the little black numbers and the pointing fingers of the minute and second hands in our clocks. We are handed time of a different nature. What truly belongs to us is able to come to us, to sit gently at our feet that have finally stopped tapping.

Each rose that comes brings me greetings from the Rose of an eternal spring. God honors me when I work, but loves me when I sing.

RABINDRANATH TAGORE

As a rule, it was the pleasure-haters who became unjust. w.h. auden

SIMPLE PLEASURES

The kindness of giving others simple pleasures is a pleasure itself. The meal cooked with love will not be easily forgotten. Soul food is more than a taste. It satisfies in ways that cannot be put into words. The gift of an armful of aromatic herbs and beautiful flowers will lift another's spirits. We are meant to have pleasure with our senses, to celebrate the joy that can be felt there. "Do you have a body?" asks Kabir. "Don't sit on the porch! Go out and walk in the rain!"

Since the soul and the body are best friends why can't our minds be taught to be kind and find simple loving ways to let them join? The best way for that to happen is to embrace our sensuality: our skin-knowing, our taste-savoring, and our scent-delighting. The days we honor the ways in which our bodies open to delight are days that remain with us longer than others.

Eating a ripe pear slowly, are we not eating the whole of summer's gifts: sun and rain, pollination, budding, flowering, fruiting? It can be experienced and tasted in a single bite, if we don't hurry, and if we fully appreciate every mouthful. Things are fleeting, yet in the moment of deep savoring, we sense something eternal.

The paradox is that this way of appreciation brings us to less consumption and more gratefulness. We give ourselves to the experience. In all addictions and overuse of our sensuality, we are not giving to ourselves. We are taking. There is only greed and no mutuality. In the end, we are consumed in our consuming.

When we give ourselves and each other thoughtful sensual pleasures, we create an atmosphere of kindness. Together we experience what is good in life. Our senses are filled with delight.

The key, however, is the word simple. In simple pleasures given and received, we reach into what is pure, what is refined, and what will feed us in an essential, unmixed way. We know that in this simple pleasing of one another, the heart is honored. The Creator's generosity is honored. Gratefully and mindfully partaking in simple, sensual gifts, we live in praise.

REFLECTIONS

ON KINDNESS

TOWARD OTHERS

How should I live?
Live welcoming to all.

MECHTILD OF MAGDEBURG

HOSPITALITY

Every moment is a time for hospitality. *Now* is always the welcome mat at the threshold of inclusion. How do we live a life of welcome? The truth is that we do not welcome everything. We shut the door on pain, fear, disgust, strangeness, and every manner of thing we don't even know.

It is easy to feel kindness toward that which appeals. Kindness to that which is abhorrent is hard to learn. We need to surrender to the fact that we will never be able to really welcome what frightens us. It requires us to surrender and be vulnerable to the quick.

If anything, God is inclusive beyond imagining. The enormity and diversity of God's creation is proof of that. It will never come to an end. It is ongoing, happening every second—a resounding *YES* to all that can be, good or bad (from our point of view). Who then are we to shut the door?

Can we ask for the courage to open our doors a crack? Can we note when we are about to slam the door and lock it tight? Even a moment of hesitation will offer asylum to our reactivity. Imagine being able, on the spot, to confess, *I am scared. I am unwilling*. Can we be hospitable to our frightened, homeless selves?

That doesn't mean we have opened the door. It doesn't mean we have slammed the door either. We are just sitting there on the muddy welcome mat, giving our frightened selves a little kindness. We are being caring long enough for reactivity to subside a little...perhaps a minute, perhaps years. The welcome mat invites us to enroll in the school of imperfection. There we are both teachers and students. We are learning to be human, and that is what God wants of us. Accepting our humanity is the kindness that will welcome even the difficult.

The air, blowing everywhere,
serves all creatures.

HILDEGARD OF BINGEN

KINDNESS IN, KINDNESS OUT

Can we think of kindness as a way to breathe? Our lungs fill and empty without our having to make them do so. However, when we attend to our breathing, something changes. The air seems to fill us more than otherwise, and it also releases us, empties us, so that we can take another deep inhalation. Paying attention to breathing has been classical in most spiritual practices. Making the breath a vehicle for kindness is therefore not strange but natural.

When we join our wish to be kind with awareness of the breath, every inhalation opens us to receive kindness like manna from the universe. And with every exhalation, we send kindness back to whomever or whatever needs it. We do not have to be specific, but we can be. This exhalation, this kindness breath, is for anyone who can use it, or this kindness breath is for a spouse, a child, a friend, or a coworker, etc. Our lungs will become bellows for kindness transmission.

Can we find natural times to pause and breathe kindness into the world for our own sakes, for others, and for the environment? This practice is so simple and is available at any moment. To link it, however, with something we already do helps to make it a habit. After a meal, for instance, is a natural time. A minute before we engage the ignition of our car can be a minute to ignite kindness. When we go to bed or first thing in the morning are also good times. For each person there will be periods in the day where exhaling kindness can easily fit. We will be the first beneficiaries of this practice. It can hold us steady in times when it would otherwise be hard to be kind. We are all breathing air that everyone and everything that has ever been alive has breathed. This common air can be graced with kindness. It is a prayer to do so, and it will slowly make us breathtaking.

*A touch is enough
to let us know we're not
alone in the universe...*

ADRIENNE RICH

THE WARMTH IN OUR HANDS

I was touched by that, we say, and we mean that
feelings were awakened in us the way strings
on a guitar might come to life and vibrate when
they are stroked. As infants we would wither
and die without being touched. Our skin is the
largest organ in the body. It is the interface between us and everything else.

There is so much we have to handle and do.
Our touch becomes purposeful. We are get-
ting the job done! Someone in a nursing home
handled this way might feel their skin shrink-
ing when touched as if they were merely a job
to be done and over with. We need to reclaim

our hands and their warmth from the mind that drives and demands that an endless list of things be done. We know the difference between someone touching us in a harmful way and when we are touched in a loving manner. Custody of our hands is a tender discipline. To touch with reverence is a profound kindness we can offer others.

How do we do that? First, we can realize it took millions of years for an opposing thumb to evolve so that our hands could grasp. We are recipients of the evolution of trillions of lives. A hand that can hold is a miracle, and we have two of them. We can grasp, hold, and caress. Could it be that evolution wants us not just to survive but also to learn to touch with awareness and care?

There is an amazing kindness in a pair of warm hands. They can gentle another human being who is afraid or lonely. They can assure a state of friendship. They can protect, guide, and teach. They can bless. No wonder that the image of hands brought palm to palm in front of the heart is known as a sacred gesture of both prayer and recognition. The gesture wordlessly says, *Namaste, I see the divinity in you.*

*To be religious is to give
your life so that the world may be
more beautiful, more just, more at peace;
it is to prevent egotistical and self-
serving ends from disrupting
this harmony of the whole.*

ARTURO PAOLI

THE LITTLE STEP BACKWARD

An artist will step back from a painting on the easel in order to see it better. Up close it can be a wild mix of lines, colors, textures, and empty spaces. There is so much to embellish or to eliminate. To have perspective on what belongs is to take a little step backwards.

Our lives are the canvas we are painting, and they are filled with responsibilities, with people, with tasks and longings. Close up, we deal as best we can. There is both immediacy and exhaustion in the way we have to respond moment to moment. To step back from all that now and then is a little bit of self-kindness. It is also a kindness to others and to the situations we find ourselves in. We may be needed, but we are not indispensable. As someone humorously put it, "We are not God's only resource."

This step is not about rest or withdrawal, but about regaining perspective so we can see the whole. Perhaps we can think of this little step as a courtesy. It is an inner acknowledgment that we don't see the whole picture. Before we blurt something out in a quick unthinking response, can we pull back a moment to sense if what we are about to say furthers anything? Before we leap in to help, can we step back to see if we are enabling or ennobling?

For most of us this step will not feel like kindness or even courtesy. It may feel like discipline and constraint. To *not do*, however, can be one of the kindest things we can be about. How will we know if we don't step back and gain perspective? Our *not doing* may turn out to make room for someone else *to do*. It could be the most important, loving kindness we can be about, especially with grown children who need to fly with their own wings. Stepping back, we make room for understanding and room for others. Stepping back, we make room for Spirit to guide us. Stepping back is actually a little dance step that lets us step forward again in a more graceful way.

*Three things in human life
are important: the first is to be kind;
the second is to be kind; and the
third is to be kind.*

HENRY JAMES

THE SILENCE THAT SPEAKS

We use words every day, and somewhere we know that in even casual use, words have an enormous power to hurt or to help. Take gossip, for instance. It slips out of us like a little newsreel, and we pass things along that may or may not be true. It is such a deep human habit that we don't even notice the potential harm we may be creating.

In a sense we are in a children's game called "telephone." In it, the person who begins the chain of events whispers something quietly to the person next to them. That person then whispers it to the next person, and so on. At the end, what was first said is revealed, and often, with chuckles, what was last heard is a complete distortion of the original message.

Whenever we can catch ourselves in such a gossip chain and are able to resist the impulse to join in, we will be speaking volumes. Instead of the unconscious use of words, could we decide to say one kind thing to a person some time during the day? It is like handing them a bouquet of flowers. There will be fragrance in the air.

In another context, it takes kindness of heart to resist correcting someone we are with. We may very well be right about the correction, but not helpful in our timing. Words that carry clout need a chance to be heard. The person who is to receive our words needs to be considered. If we blurt things out willy-nilly with self-appointed urgency and no sense of timing, we'll need correction too.

In the beginning was the Word, the energy,

that vibration that brought creation into being. Our words are vibes for goodwill or ill will and everything in between. They are powerful tools of creation and destruction. When kindness is the underlying vibration, then good always comes into being. We have that human gift to voice goodness into the world. May we use that gift with great care.

Do your little bit of good where you are; it's those little bits of good put together that overwhelm the world.

DESMOND TUTU

A WORK IN PROGRESS

When we accept that our lives are always unfinished and that, even so, they are of immense beauty, we'll be able to live one little step at a time. If that small step is valued for itself, for the tiny, humble adventure that it is, we'll not seek what is beyond us. We'll be glad of the journey and let the destination take care of itself.

Even lives that are full of challenge, despair, and pain have great value and a haunting beauty. We are who we are, because we have undergone the difficulties that somehow belong to us. When kindness resides in us, the world is lit with a soft light. It is no accident that the word kindness begins with the word *kin*. Under the auspices of kindness, everything is illuminated as somehow kin to us, though we don't know how. There's no way to be outside reality although we often make strangers of ourselves and of others. Day by day we need only to take our next step into *kin*ship.

We already know that everyone is vulnerable, and that change is the way of it all. But when universal kinship is understood, we learn to be careful. How we are with others is really how we are with ourselves. The painful lives of others will mark us, as will the joyful ones. Lessons learned are not for us alone. In the word *yours* is the word *ours*. In these days, kindness matters more than it ever has before. It gives loving permission for a better world to evolve that is not yet visible.

In the morning, when our feet touch the floor, we step into a new day. In that very moment we can decide to walk into a day of kinship. Forgive the pun; the bottoms of our feet will become all soul. Kindness is always from the bottom up. It inhabits lowly places, the ordinary things we handle, and the loving drudgery we might have to suffer for the sake of another. When we stand and walk in kindness, we are immediately grounded, by earth, humus, humility, and humanness. To live kindness is a journey of immense worth and will continue beyond the span of our lives.

*A single act of kindness throws
out roots in all directions, and the roots
spring up and make new trees.*

AMELIA EARHART

THE KINDNESS OF A TREE

There are times when, if we are as sturdy and still as trees, we can be experienced as the presence of kindness for another being. Kindness then is not a doing, but a steady, rooted presence. In that presence others can find shade from whatever glaring intensity they are exposed to. They can lean on us, and we will not go away. Neither will we take upon ourselves the challenge that belongs to those who are leaning on us. We are simply there, perhaps for the first time in someone's life, or the one they come to often for rest and solace.

In those situations the temptation to speak and figure things out for another must be resisted. This is true also for the temptation to offer other kinds of assistance. The deep kindness here is to trust in the capacity of the person who has turned to us, to believe in *them*.

The kindness of a tree is not easy to develop, but when we are able to offer it, we will find how simple presence has solace and brings new strength. To offer this kindness, we ourselves must be rooted in a ground of our own. We need to have spent enough time being nourished by nature, by silence, and by trust in the deep unknown. Only then will we feel our life force rise in us like sap. We will have branched out in experience enough to have a wide perspective. We will have surrendered what we needed to in the storms and freezing cold that comes to every life. Even in shifting winds, we will be able to have a heartwood of peace from season to season.

This is a lot to offer another person, and almost always we will have the niggling doubt that our silence and presence are not enough, that we simply aren't giving anything at all. Even half of the above would do. Having received kindness like this from someone else, we will sense that even a little stillness and rootedness is a wonderful gift. Then we might also sense that, like trees that give off their oxygen, our presence gives off something that is needed. We are giving what we are, and that is the greatest gift we can ever give.

The shutters of my mind habitually flip open and click shut, and these little snaps form into patterns I arrange for myself. The opposite of this inattention is love, is the honoring of others in a way that grants them the grace of their own autonomy and allows mutual discovery.

ANNE TRUITT

OF BEAUTY MADE

Beauty is in the eye of the beholder we are told. That will color all experience won't it? To invite beauty's presence is to have an artist's palette inside us, with every imaginable color since it is in our beholding that we discover beauty. Apart from that, beauty simply *is*, without theories or explanations. It needs no beholding. It is this beauty that we already are.

If the heart were a simple mirror of kindness, it would reflect beauty without effort. It would reflect even the dreadful in a manner that truthfully told the whole, stark beauty of it all. To have no preconceived notion of what is beautiful is a profound thing and it requires from us a deep respect for what is. The kindest people that exist are those who do just that. For them, beauty cascades around them, spills over every concrete surface they walk upon.

It is audacious to say that we can make anything beautiful without telling lies. Take one rusty can with some leftover, greasy contents still clinging to the bottom. When we let it be as it is, allow it to catch light from the sun streaming through the window, we might perhaps see glistening surfaces, the elegance of gray, feathery mold, and the rightness of rust as a color. We would not shrink in disgust from the details we notice. We'd let the can just be there with us and reflect it back to itself. That process can be understood to be a part of beauty.

Seeing beauty is a sweet, daily task. It requires nothing but a ready heart that meets the world with kindness. Finding one, small, perhaps lonely seeming thing, and taking it to heart, spending a moment with it for no purpose at all except to be there side by side, is a deep secret. Something will begin to shine. It has to. Beauty will out whenever we give something our full attention.

When we gaze at our surroundings with all cultural, personal, or other associations forgotten, what we see will shimmer with life, with the strange tenderness that flows through everything. We, too, will naturally be made beautiful.

It is impossible, I think,
taking our nature into consideration,
that anyone who fails to realize
that he or she is favored by God
should have the courage necessary
for doing great things.

ST. TERESA OF AVILA

REFLECTIONS
ON THE LIGHT
OF KINDNESS

LIVING A GOOD QUESTION

Kindness practice is dynamic, often spontaneous, rising up simply to meet the moment.
But sometimes how to be kind in a situation
needs discernment. We have to consider what
we will say or do. To be kind in those situations may need mulling.

A question that cuts through our confusion
is a tool of the heart, not a scalpel. Here is one
that will serve us well when asked and given
time to be heard. An answer will come that is
not only based on good sense, but also on the
wisdom of the heart and gut, that is to say, on
loving intuition. The question is this: *What
serves Life here?*

We may be faced with a slew of choices, but
when we ask that question, we will sense what
furthers Life itself, not anyone's preferred or
obligatory choice. In choosing what serves
Life, we are mysteriously given the means to
do so. The Love of God always serves Life, and
so we find we can align ourselves with that

power—even if at that time the cost might be high, and our contribution seemingly small.

Hearing the answer to that question is an act of kindness itself. We are not just reacting. We are responding. Intuition is very body-centered. Something will feel more right than something else. We will experience a sense of relief when we choose to serve Life. Our own needs will not be left out of the equation either.

This question can be a daily prayer question. *How can I serve Life today?* When we follow through on the answer we are given, the way will be shown to us. Whether we are in crisis or in joy, we will be steered. We will be spiritually guided, and the outcome will not be up to us.

I know well that heaven
and earth and all creation are great,
generous and beautiful and good...
God's goodness fills all his creatures
and all his blessed work full, and endlessly
overflows in them...God is everything
that is good, as I see it, and the goodness
which everything has is God.

JULIAN OF NORWICH

THE WELL INSIDE

From what well deep inside is kindness drawn? The answer is not easy. Perhaps other people who emulated kindness inspired us, and we want to be like them. We may have received a kindness that brought us out of a personal darkness, and we want to give kindness back to the world. We might simply have been taught courtesy in our youth, and the habit grew into a kindliness of being.

It is very daring to believe that we, by simply being born human, have been given kindness as a deep well inside us. That is like discovering a clear spring in a parched field. *Who me? I have that?* More astonishing yet is that the spring keeps brimming with fullness no matter how often we use it.

What if we dared to peek into that mystery the way you might peer down into a well? We'd see the holding stones. We'd see how the light is able to go just so far down. If we dropped a small stone in the well, we'd hear it plop as if from very far away when it reached the water.

Here is a secret. There truly is a well inside us that we will never know or see the bottom of. It has living water in it. The well and the water is God's trust in us, a trust in our frail humanity.

To truly believe that we are trusted will make us thirst for living water. It will make us want to draw from the well, draw and spill out kindness with abandon, with happy craziness. The well is deep. There is always more living water to draw from. It is God's well. God's trust in our capacity is never-ending. That trust fills the well. If we do not cut the cord, we can draw from the well, not with our confidence, but with God's confidence in us. We can pour.

The soul loves the body.

MEISTER ECKHART

BEING SOMEBODY

So many of us disparage our bodies. We think we are too fat, too thin, too tall, too short—not blond and smooth-skinned—not the right shade, not right in some way. We have forgotten that the body we have is, first and foremost, a gift. Nothing is a gift until it is received.

Thinking of the body as a gift is a necessary kindness practice. Our bodies need care, not misuse. They will have aches and pains soon enough as we age.

Can we understand that in every cell of our bodies there is light and intelligence? Can we marvel that we have a bone structure that allows us to walk upright? Can we appreciate that our skin breathes, as do our lungs? The body is amazing. It is a temple. Thinking of our bodies as temples, it is harder to want to trash them. They are the breathing, living sanctuaries of our lives. When we wash our bodies, when we clothe them, let it not be to impress, but to care for our earthly home, our abiding place. Our bodies are with us as long as we are alive. Can we say that about anything else that is of this earth?

The way we treat our body being is often the way we treat others. Lack of self-respect and self-care is then projected outward to others. Neglect invites neglect. If kindness is to be the direction of our spiritual practice, then care of our bodies matters a great deal. Nothing about it can be dismissed as irrelevant. Food, sleep, exercise, hours at work, etc., have to be considered and balanced. Seen rightly, these can be kindness practices. They are the gift of being somebody; the very one God has given life to. *Just to be is a blessing. Just to live is holy*, wrote Abraham Heschel. It is in the way we carry our bodies, the way we care for them, the way we share them, that kindness will shine through.

Men do change, and change
comes like a little wind that ruffles
the curtains at dawn, and it comes
like the stealthy perfume of
wildflowers hidden in the grass.

JOHN STEINBECK

THE AFTER LIGHT

We have encounters that make no impression
on us, and we have encounters that affect us
deeply. They have an *after light,* so to speak.
There is actually nothing that does not have
light. Even darkness has light of a different
order.

When we look at a color field that is red, and
we gaze at it for a solid minute we will discover that we are also seeing green. We can call

the green the red's *after light*. Red and green are the colors of traffic lights that direct us to stop or go.

Our actions and our words also have *after lights*. When we can't sense the impact an encounter had on us, we can stop and allow the *after light* to reveal itself. Sometimes we will be in situations that appear difficult and unpleasant, perhaps even terrifying. We see red, and it stops us cold. Later another light might emerge and show us a new way to proceed. That possibility is a greening one, and we could call it kindness.

If we would embrace the idea that the *after light* is a deep vibrational truth, we would be more able to be patient in hard times. We would be able to trust that kindness can be present at all times. It is a continuous invitation to live with paradoxes, with mysteries that don't reveal themselves easily. Looking for the kindness *after light* can become nourishing, if we will let things emerge as they can without undue insistence.

Pressuring ourselves or others is not kind. Kindness flourishes where permission exists. Can we learn to trust that in dark times an *after light* exists and will shine in time? That light will not be overcome.

You must make the most strenuous efforts. Throughout this life, you can never be certain of living long enough to take another breath.

HUANG PO

THE GIFT IN LIMITATIONS

In every life there are limitations, parameters within which we live. One is the body. We have a strong constitution or we don't. Another is our intelligence. We are bright or we are not so bright. Perhaps we were raised in affluence and possibility, or we were raised with a minimum of choices. We were given a set of limits at the outset.

Of course, we know that limitations can be stretched by hard work and intention, and they can also be accepted. We can learn to live within them and find possibilities there that may become of great worth to us. They may even set us free.

Many have heard from people with chronic diseases like Parkinson's Disease, that they are grateful for their condition. Within that limitation they were able to grow personally and found the disease to ultimately bring great kindness from others and a new meaning to life.

What if we thought of a limitation as being like a womb? By stopping any hostile feelings we have toward our limiting circumstances, we can be conceived again. We can begin to experience the kindness inherent in the limitation. We can sense what there is *for* us in the circumstance, and what can grow with our participation. Something new can be born that may even help others.

The bottom line is that underneath every circumstance whether we are fit, emotionally connected, financially stable or not, we will be limited by the span of our lives. We will die. When knowing this can be seen as a gift, we will appreciate almost everything we have now, however big or small it is. It will inspire us to live all that we can live.

Good fences make good neighbors.

ROBERT FROST

WHOLENESS IN BOUNDARIES

Boundaries are different from limits, though they are also a kind of limitation. Having strong boundaries can be an elegant way to be kind to ourselves and to others. Boundaries have everything to do with integrity. They help us know what we will participate in, and what we will refuse. Boundaries do not need to be immovable, but without them we are wishy-washy, overrun by demands made by others or by unrealistic expectations we heap upon ourselves.

Stone walls along the fields in New England can be truly beautiful. There, the art of choosing how one stone fits with another can be seen as high art. That these walls held up for hundreds of years without mortar is a wonder. An open field with a sturdy stone wall is a spiritual icon.

Back when the land was wilderness, and a field was to be cleared, every stone that was dug up was taken to the edge of that clearing. When we dig up what is in the way of our inner truth, we have the makings of integrity and a good boundary. Integrity is a hard-won thing. It takes years to develop. To recognize the impediments in our being and to dig them out is to develop conscience. Let's say hardness of heart is something that we want to dig up. Perhaps being stubborn is another, or irritability and unwillingness to accommodate other people is a third.

Farmers in the past didn't throw away the stones they dug up. They found a new use for them in walls that made good boundaries. So, too, when we clear our inner field, we don't discard what was once there. We treat it with respect. We let it be seen as part of our wholeness, rethought and reconstructed to serve in a more useful way.

If someone asks my abode I reply:
"The east edge of The Milky WAY."

RYOKAN

NORTH STAR PERSPECTIVE

If kindness is a north star to navigate by, then
no matter what events take place in our lives
they are ultimately meant for our good. That
doesn't mean we will be spared suffering. No
life is without it.

One way we suffer is to rail at suffering
itself, to resist and reject it. We refuse what
has come to us to live with, and to live through.
We are not willing to be transformed by what
life has brought us. We just see ourselves with
more scars the way a breadboard is scored. We

remain wooden. Another way to suffer is to grow into the perspective that everything we experience is somehow essential for us. When suffering is a dark night, then kindness is the starlight that permeates our pain. Our suffering is specific to our situation, neither random nor a form of punishment. Whatever it is that we must live with and through is somehow meant for our good.

With this perspective, we are asked to believe that Life is a school of learning, and every part of suffering that we take up consciously becomes light in both senses of the word— weightless and luminous. Understanding this is knowing the earth and all that is in it, including us, evolved from the stuff of stars and that our spiritual task and gift is to shine brightly in whatever way we can.

A large step we can take to grow into this perspective is to embrace our pain as much as we embrace our joy. Our pain may be a tough teacher, whose methods seem harsh but whose love is generous. In learning this, we become witnesses in our lives. We are not seeking anymore. We are learning deeply from the moment, finding and slowly learning that *now* is enough. We can grow to want what we have.

This is living beyond *me first*. With a larger perspective we take in the world around us better, perhaps seeing how sunlight, that golden radiance from our star, enters our rooms, and fills them with light. We'll see the way birds spread their wings and play in the wind. It may be that we'll hear trees sing together. We will know that we are in and part of all of that is and that it makes us whole.

For to stay wholly with each moment
is the death of the ego, who lives always
in either the past or future.

HELEN LUKE

DYING OFTEN

What a kindness it is to die a little each day; that is, to not insist that things should be different from the way they are. It is to be with our own experience with a sense of reverence even though it may be dull, painful, or very ordinary. It is to live neither in the past nor in the future. We can easily be aware of this. *Remember when* is full of nostalgia. *It will be great when* is leaping ahead to some fictional arrival.

Being fully alive is only possible when we lend our presence to the present. This truth has been said and written countless times. We know that it's so, but allowing ourselves to be present to the present is not easy. In essence it is being available to conscious transformation, and ultimately to the experience of vulnerability. Being truly present, we are defenseless. We will be affected by whatever is happening at the moment both inside of ourselves and outside of ourselves. It is being genuinely alive. The false self wants assurance and protection.

The essential self consents to the moment.

Whenever we manage to be truly present, we are in training for transition. Reliving the past or imagining the future, we are stuck in virtual reality. We could think of it like surfing an app. We are removed, viewing our lives as if on a screen rather than being alive *in them*. When we really show up and participate, we feel experience and change very intimately. It touches us. We sense how nothing stays the same. Our lives are moving every single second. We realize that we are in a continual flow, a continual transformative process, and a continual disappearance of what was. This is happening to everything and everyone around us.

As the earth spins at a hurtling pace, though we do not perceive it here on the ground, our body systems are breaking down and building up at an amazing speed. The only response of any value in this perpetual change is to be kind, to know we have no permanence, nor any power to stop the flow. But we have the means to be gentle, to be aware and kind in the daily mystery of dying to live.

*Tenderness and kindness are not signs
of weakness and despair, but manifestations
of strength and resolution.*

KAHLIL GIBRAN

BEING A BRIDGE

A bridge is a span over something—a railroad track, a flowing river, or a deep valley. It is in the structure of a bridge to carry weight and to tolerate tension. What a good metaphor a bridge is for kindness, when something deep and conflicted opens up before us that we must live, transcend, and cross.

There are always at least two sides in a conflict, and also a terrain between them, full of rocks and underbrush. That terrain will often be ignored in the conflict. It doesn't get to state its case, while metaphorical boots trample on its right to exist. An enormous, quiet strength is needed to be aware of the entire situation.

To not choose sides, to tolerate the anger hurled at us when we do not choose sides, is to be a bridge of kindness. To span a great divide, there needs to be solid footing on either side. When we can hear each point of view without reactivity, we construct a necessary footing, so to speak. Hard things need to be said and heard fully. This takes endurance and the willingness to respect and bear the tension. Such subtle strength drives a stable footing into the ground for something new to be constructed. It is the only way a willingness to meet in the middle can take place.

This may take years, or it may take only an hour. In either case, it is to participate in suffering, rather than to fix, ignore, or control it. It is honoring the common pain. To be a bridge for others we must bridge the chasms inside ourselves, too, and not project our unsolved difficulties on others. That is the mystery of kindness. To listen, to listen again and again, is to hear not just one side and then the other, but both sides and the in-between simultaneously. This takes spiritual muscle. Acceptance of the multi-sidedness of things is fierce strength. When everyone retains their dignity and gains some of what they were fighting for, we have succeeded. Bridges are made so that not only we but *all* others can also move on in their journeys.

The best and most beautiful things
in the world cannot be seen, nor touched,
but are felt in the heart.

HELEN KELLER

ALONE TOGETHER

Every day and every hour we are silently connected to everything. But we do not live in awareness of this companionship that is so immense and so inclusive. Though vast and yet intimate, this interconnectedness leaves us to develop our own ways. We are alone together, and together alone—a paradox and also a liberty filled with kindness.

Our minds have a hard time holding on to the awareness of this huge connection. Since we cannot actually see or encompass in a lived knowing way the infinite hugeness that we are, we often feel alone in a universe that couldn't care less. In another moment, however, when beauty or kindness touches us with kid gloves, we are brought into participation. Alone becomes together again.

What is it that makes this happen? Is it not awareness? Someone or something becomes so real to us that we are brought into *wonder*. A lilting song, a beckoning scent, a loveliness of gesture, a beguiling smile, or a luminous tear brings us out of self-preoccupation. We are brought to the big self that all of us are, and we are reunited for a moment.

Part of kindness practice is to dwell in, and with, whatever arises, entering into *wonder* as a life script. Birders rise early and go out in all kinds of weather. They travel to faraway places to see birds they have not yet seen. They are dedicated to discovery. We can be *wonder-watchers* with eyes that see and ears that hear moments of beauty and meaning. We are ready to discover and to be open to what can only be known in the heart.

Some birds are so tiny that they are barely seen. So, too, some moments are so small we have to bring all that we are to be able to sense them. That manner of sensing is kindness itself. What we look for gazes back at us. Discovery becomes recovery, and we are once again in the heart of *wonder*.

Kindness is not an art. It is a lifestyle.
ANTHONY DOUGLAS

RANDOM ACTS

Kindness, like blessing, is experienced in a particular moment in and for a particular person or situation. Though seeming random, surfacing here and there, yet it lands squarely in a definite somewhere at a specific moment in time.

Kindness is aroused in us when we notice, when we see/feel/hear and cannot stop ourselves from acting on behalf of another in empathy or joy. Our hearts simply cannot help themselves. We join with that which we have witnessed. We can call this random, but looking more deeply, we will see that kindness is a source of life that undergirds everything.

We can come to know that, yes, we are particular agents of kindness, but that the kindness we offer has its wellspring beyond us. We are simply conduits. As conduits, however, we are also flooded and graced in the process. Joined to what or to whom is in need of kindness, we somehow become kindness. It happens by itself.

Kindness arises in us not only when empathy has been awakened in us. It also surfaces as play. *What spontaneous fun will take place when we prepay the toll for the car behind us? What mischief will arise when we leave a gift without a message at someone's door for the sheer surprise of it? What spontaneous compliment can make another person's day?*

Are these random acts, or is it kindness itself bubbling up inside us? When we sense that any act of kindness we engage in, or are the recipients of, arises from a place Beyond, we may be more confident in extending it and receiving it. Kindness has no limit. The more we are in its flow, the more we will have of it, and the more we will be carried by its life-giving current.

It is known that even in chaos there are patterns. Random as it may seem, living in the kindness current we will be in an unending pattern that serves life. Kindness is like a spring of living water. It needs us to draw from it. It needs us to pour.

*Be kind, for everyone you meet
is fighting a hard battle.*

PLATO

911

We respond with kindness in emergencies. Because they are emergencies, we go full out. Something about our own need to survive and identification with the pain of others moves us to help, to be there in whatever way we can.

What if we were to live this way without the clanging bell of the fire truck, the siren of the ambulance, or the immense horror of destruction? What if we really understood that every day the world is rescued by kindness, by small and constant acts of goodness that are everywhere, and that go unnoticed? What if kindness was already viral?

Pour water into a clear glass. Hear the sound of it pouring. Drink slowly. Taste the water. It has the unique taste of itself. Put your hand gently on the sponge. Turn on the tap and wash the glass of water with water. Feel the warmth of the water on your hands.

Feel the intimacy of these acts. Why not give kindness to others, to inanimate things, and to the most ordinary tasks? We live so much in a state of emergency. Our tasks overwhelm and bury us. We need to be rescued by the presence of kindness. This is what will keep us from destroying our bodies, our friends, our homes with activities and goods that will only satisfy us for a moment and never fulfill us.

Every one of our breaths feeds the trees, and they return the favor. Together we are this earth and its elements. Every self-offering allows something to live more fully, although we will never know how. That finally does not matter. Small acts of simple kindness are like taking the last straw off the camel's back before it breaks. Then the journey can somehow continue over vast deserts, if need be.

We rescue small things from oblivion with moments of awareness. That means being aware of continual emergence without emergency. It is to live in kindness, blessed by small miracles of connection with nature, with others, with ordinary things that, when tended to, lift the last straws and conspire to heal the world.

Every grain of dust has a wonderful soul.

JOAN MIRÓ

LOVING THE EARTH

Everything that is thrums with divinity. As Meister Eckhart wrote, "Every creature is a word of God and is a book about God." Can we learn to wear glasses that would allow us to see this dimension and the wonder of it? The earth itself needs our tenderness. We call it Mother Earth. Mothers need love as much as children do, and if we were able to see two truths at once, we might begin to think of earth as a child, too, that needs our care if it is to sustain life.

In a desert, a living tree is a miracle. Every tree and plant is a miracle, something to revere, for our species has destroyed so much. We see the smokestacks that belch black clouds. We witness the mountains of plastic that we are having more and more difficulty finding a place to bury. It will take eons to break the plastic down. Taking action is now of huge importance. We can make our carbon footprint smaller, our waste less, our consumption reasonable. And though our little bit is so tiny in comparison to what is needed, it is still important.

Some meditation practices ask us to walk mindfully. Could the soles of our feet be souls? Can we step on the ground at least once a day with the intention of walking our talk and to do something for our planet?

Treating one living thing with kinship will in essence be worship, and an act of praise. Can we help in a communal garden, or have one of our own? Can we tend one plant in our home, and sense that it reflects something about God? Consciousness itself is energy. Awareness is a current that enhances what it is aware of. When we speak to our house-plants lovingly, they grow stronger and green-er. Such care given makes us care-full. We get more than we give. This is a central truth about kindness.

How long will it take, and how many of us will be a quorum that can bring about rever-ence for our planet? Let us begin soul walking and loving the earth for itself and not just for what it gives. Let us trust that awareness is a force, and that care can send kindness down to the magma.

To rejoice in another person's joy
is like being in heaven.

MEISTER ECKHART

PLAY

Praise and play dance with each another. They are very close in the human spirit. To feel, know, and daily experience how kindness is everywhere around us and in us, is to live in praise. To notice the many-sided ways that kindness touches us is to be both in praise and in play. We will never see kindness apart from specific circumstances and specific people, but we can notice where it is.

Kindness is dressed up in many costumes and plays many parts in our lives. It shines its light into every corner where it is allowed. In short, it plays with us, if we will play with it. Perhaps we can think of kindness as a form of mutual radiance. When we find it, we are also found. It seems right to end this small book about kindness with a riff of aphorisms acknowledging the blessings that kindness is. No one thing will ever capture it. But we can play with looking for where it is, not hide and seek, but seek and find.

❧ In the mirror of kindness, we can bear
to see all of ourselves, inside and out,
even what we do not like.

❧ The hand of kindness is subtle.
It has a long and tender reach.

❧ Hearing the deep cry of the world,
kindness gathers our tears.

❧ Kindness has a way of walking
in everybody's shoes.

❧ Kindness is the friend that knows
the truth about us and gives us back
to ourselves.

❧ Kindness wears no watch and has all
the time in the world.

❧ To be kind to our selves starts a
revolution not a war. It makes peace
with more things than we can fathom.

❧ Kindness is the point of the pen
that draws beauty out of us.

❧ In the kaleidoscope of kindness when
things fall apart, the pieces are the
same, but the pattern is new.

❧ When kindness enters, the walls step
back, and the house gets bigger.

❧ Sometimes kindness is silent,
a silence so sweet it enters the marrow
of our bones.

❧ With ears to the ground, kindness
counts the steps we have taken
to mend the ache of the world.

❧ Kindness is like yeast. It leavens
and lifts what is heavy.

❧ To forgive another is the kindness
we give to ourselves.

❧ Even with the tiniest of wagons,
   kindness can carry a big load.

❧ We can be sure that when we look for
   kindness, it is looking for us, too.

❧ How awesome to realize that
   everything we do matters! This is
   even more the truth when we act with
   kindness.

LAST WORDS

As unhelpful patterns in our lives reassert themselves, let us keep turning our life's kaleidoscope toward kindness with the perception of its infinite value. That turning will make our lives become more and more vibrant with energy. Kindness is a vast domain, a generous field, and a powerful pattern. Any occurrence whatsoever, where even a small act of kindness takes place, alters the situation. The moment's apparent limitation has been changed. A new graciousness is possible, a potential is evoked, and a new beginning has a chance to emerge.

We will never know how far small acts of kindness reach when we have been spontaneous in our responses, and forgetful of ourselves. When we align with kindness, whether consciously or instinctively, we are live-wired into the pattern that sustains life. A week consciously noticing acts of kindness by others will astound us.

May kindness color our lives with beauty

and with fresh meaning. We are kin to all that exists. It is together that we make our homes and communities places we want to love and inhabit. We are part of a great evolution of consciousness that is growing stronger, and leading humans to be more and more aware of how interconnected the web of life is. Knowing we are one, we can realize that what we do to others, we are doing to ourselves. We can learn to be more careful of our beautiful planet, of all its parts and inhabitants. In fact, there is nothing that exists that does not have life, worthiness, and its place in the majesty we share.

It may well be that cultivating kindness will save our planet for future generations. To daily and weekly share great love in little ways will make us participants in this awesome task of evolution.

Days follow nights. The moon waxes and wanes. The seasons come and go. Looking deeply, the grace of kindness will be there.

The highest form of wisdom is kindness.

THE TALMUD